Mrs Weber's Diary

Posy Simmonds, who was born in Berkshire, studied painting in Paris and graphic design at the Central School of Art and Design, London. She is married and lives in London. Besides her weekly comic strip, *The Silent Three* in the *Guardian*, she has done a wide range of freelance illustration for books, journals and newspapers including the *Observer*, the *Sun* and the *Sunday Times*.

Posy Simmonds

Mrs Weber's Diary

FONTANA/COLLINS

The Characters

1	**Edmund HEEP**	(father & whisky salesman)
2	**Jolyon HEEP**	(at secondary school)
3	**Jo HEEP**	(mother & tennis coach)
4	**Julian HEEP**	(at secondary school, founder of 'The Snotty Throttlers' pop group)
5	**Benji WEBER**	(at nursery school)
6	**George WEBER**	(father, Senior Lecturer in Liberal Studies at a polytechnic)
7	**Wendy WEBER**	(mother, ex-nurse, now writer of children's books)
8	**Pussy**	(Weber cat, neutered tom)
9	**Amanda WEBER**	(twins, at primary school)
10	**Tamsin WEBER**	
11	**Sophie WEBER**	(at secondary school)
12	**Beverley WEBER**	(at secondary school)
13	**Belinda WEBER**	(at secondary school, taking 2 'A' Levels)
14	**Stanhope WRIGHT**	(father, creative director of Beazeley & Buffin Advertising)
15	**Trish WRIGHT**	(mother, former art gallery assistant, Stanhope's 2nd wife)
16	**Willy WRIGHT**	
17	**Jocasta WRIGHT**	(art student, Stanhope's daughter from his 1st marriage)

January

<u>Friday</u>   Colinshawes' Party   8.30   (Babysitter)

Saturday   Woke late with ~~te~~ frightful hangover. Broke New Year resolution.
(George - very smug, kept his, which is to Get Up and Grab the Day
by the Balls.)
Listened to ^radio programme about ~~mutig-mat~~ mutagens damaging DNA in cells & giving
us all cancer. Kids went to local panto in Assembly Rooms.

X (Pay Milkman)
Asprin
veg.

Sunday.   Woke early. Pot Roast, but overdid the ~~fins~~ fines herbes.
After lunch, drove to Fladgewell Downs with the Wrights & the Heeps.
Girls stayed at home.

£52
×32
‾‾‾‾
104
1560
‾‾‾‾
£1,664

Tues. Washed druggets in the bath this morning. Removed
· ground-in chewing gum with carbon tetrachloride.
One guinea pig (Derek) very poorly with husky cough - not long for this
world I think. Benji very INTERESTED, so thought it a good time
to explain DEATH.

Wednesday. George's DAY OFF.

Spent day finishing children's story ready for publishers
to see on Fri.
Poor Derek shuffled off mortal coil. George explained death again
to Benji. I think it was the musty HAY myself. Disinfected hutch
with Lysol. Twins to BROWNIES.

Thurs. Waste cabbage leaves from grocer for guinea pigs + RABBIT PELLETS
✓ Ring VET. Finish Book. Bran?
✓ Bank

Fri. Appointment at publishers 11·00. Got early train to town — G dropped
me at station.

A very pregnant woman has gone into LABOUR! How lucky that Wendy was once a NURSE at St Thomas' Hospital....

QUICK! Get an AMBULANCE!

As wendy waits for a London train.....

CLEAR the WAITING ROOM! GET SOME SCISSORS!

THINKS: Thank God I've got LACES in my shoes!

Wendy delivers Mrs Pat Newby of a fine baby BOY in the waiting room, BEFORE the ambulance arrives!

After the event, Wendy is interviewed by the Evening Paper....

It was a very EASY labour.... I was a NURSE before I married, you see...

I used my SHOE LACES to tie the...

What does your HUSBAND do?

He's a Liberal Studies lecturer...and he's a house-husband...

..anyway, I wrapped the baby in a coat, to prevent HEAT LOSS...

You've got 6 children yourself, am I right?

I also WRITE children's books... in fact, I was on my way to see my publishers...

And HOW d'you feel, now?

Like a large GIN!

That evening, when Wendy gets home:

George! I'm ALL OVER the PAPER...I'm BLOODY FURIOUS! LOOK!

EVENING ECHO
EXPRESS DELIVERY FOR MOTHER OF SIX!

XPRESS DELIVERY R MOTHER OF SIX!

Oh mother! It's quicker by rail! The bundle arriving at Platform 4 was an express delivery for Mrs Patricia Newby (23)...a baby boy, born 2 weeks prematurely, at the Main Line Station this morning.

It seems Baby tired of waiting in the waiting room and signalled his arr-

and attractive mother of 6, Wendy Webber, calmed Pat during the delivery. "I've had six", said Wendy, "so I should know a bit about it!"

Shopping spree
Wendy, (36), who likes to read children's books as a hobby, is married to an arts teacher. She was on a shopping spree to

It makes my blood BOIL! This endless CONDESCENSION to WOMEN!....BIRTH as a JOKE!

NO mention of my initiative & common sense!

NO mention of my being a trained NURSE! 'Off on a SHOPPING SPREE!' MY GOD! HONESTLY!!

NO mention of how I used my SHOE LACES!

Yes, & I'm NOT an ARTS teacher... I'm a Senior Lecturer in Further Education

As a matter of interest, WHAT did you DO with your SHOE LACES?

Because of that paper's TRIVIALISING attitude to women, YOU & General Public will NEVER know how my laces helped at the BIRTH of a HUMAN BEING!

January

Wednesday — George late lecture.

Thurs.   HEADLICE at Benji's school. Told Mrs Pye it's NOTHING to be ashamed of.
Still FURIOUS with that frightful RACIST Sara Nutting. I wouldn't speak
to her ~~at~~ at ALL if she weren't so good at community fund raising.

Outside the nursery school, consternation reigns:

January

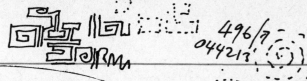

Ring Lydia / Ma / Plumber ✓✓✓

Mr Harris? 256094

Children's Xmas thank you letters

G to inspect ROOF.

496/7
044213

or. 495

Panel 1: When I was nursing, I must have seen *thousands* of *LICE*... when they're bad you get a horrible condition... *Plica Polonica*...

Panel 2: Nowadays, you get *SUPERLICE*... which are *resistant* to *insecticides*... very *WORRYING!*

Panel 3: Actually, you catch *lice* from hair that isn't *brushed a lot*, ...they don't like being disturbed, you see.

Panel 4: ...and they like it best behind the *EAR*, where it's nice & warm.... But I mustn't stand here gossiping......

Panel 5:
That Wendy knows a lot about *lice*.

Well, she's had *experience* of them

She says she's seen *1000's* in her time... no smoke without fire, I say

Fancy... so now we *know*..

Hmm, she always does look a bit *scruffy*...

but fancy her giving us *NITS!*

February

Wednesday: Snowed again. Burst pipe outside kitchen. Spend morning ringing the plumber — eventually Mrs Harris answers and says I'm the 37th burst pipe of the day. He won't come until Friday.

George working on his lecture in the bedroom — but couldn't concentrate as kept hearing DRIPPING noises on ceiling.   Went out & inspected roof with my binoculars.

Kids back early from school — bored & LETHARGIC. Suggest the therapy of ACTION — we cut up old durrie to lag pipes with.

Saturday. BEVERLEY drove us all MAD! She has to learn Macbeth /3 witches scene
        by heart for Monday. She spent the whole day SINGING it to the
tune of HERNANDO'S HIDEAWAY (as a sort of aide memoire?)
    e.g. WHEN shall WE three meet A-GAIN,
        In THUNder, LIGHTning or in RAIN etc etc etc

Sunday ALL younger ones sang 'Hernando's Hideaway' throughout the DAY.
        Could murder the lot.

8.00 Colinshawes to supper. Belinda had a date — very SULKY.
I wonder if she's on the Pill. Malcolm Muggeridge once said you could always TELL, by a deathly complexion & lacklustre eye.

B's complexion too coated in blusher.

My parents really are PEASANTS!

They look SO SCRUFFY & UNKEMPT...they NEVER buy things that LAST...

Belinda's reverie is interrupted by her boyfriend's arrival....

Mum, Dad...this is Johnny Macniece

Hi! Have some home-made PLONK!

er...NO thanks awfully.

Typical! They're always pressing ALCOHOL on you

Off you go, kids, & have a BALL!

So that's your little homestead, Belinda. Most QUAINT!

Not for long! I'm getting out, when I leave school!

This area used to be really O.K. till my parents' lot turned it into an URBAN VILLAGE

I'm SICK of lentils, old denim, Batik prints ...my parents' obsession with SEX...& their endless rapping about the boring old SIXTIES....

...when DAD joined student sit ins & Mum was a FLOWER CHILD & EARTH-MOTHER...

My parents are SO IRRESPONSIBLE -they don't care WHO I go out with.. WHERE I go...they don't care about my school work

..They don't care about ANYTHING!

Same with mine - they think the world owes them a living.

Meanwhile, at HOME:

Belinda really should be working for her A LEVELS.

But we don't believe in forcing her to stay in... she must learn to make her own discipline...

And we never pry into her private life...we're NOT SPIES...we trust her, don't we, George?

We don't want her to have any of the HANG-UPS we had about WORK & SEX...

When I THINK of how MY parents were! "Your HAIR! Those awful CLOTHES! You think the world owes you a living ...!"

Gosh Yes! I had to face INQUISITIONS!

"Where've you been? What did you do? Who did you meet?"

Belinda just doesn't know what she's missing!

February

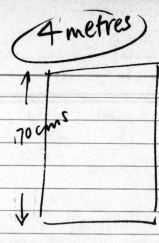

Blind Kit
Stiffener
UHU glue

3lbs mince

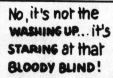

bivouac
123–125 WELLINGTON STREET, LONDON W.13

:— 001.20
:— 003.50
:— 008.45
FEB·21☊223083 :A 013·15 **T**

ebruary

Toile de Jouy

March

Tuesday — Jocasta W. came over with some illustrations for my book.
Thought she'd rather OVERDONE the atmosphere of the high rise estate
— a bit squalid. But she'd drawn SAL very well — & Sal's MUM. Hope
Walmer & Willox like them. Strange that Belinda's friendly with Jocasta —
they're both so different. B. thinks of nothing but her appearance & MEN.

March

Jocasta couldn't care less about either

I suppose J is useful for buying drinks in the Pub — also she's plain
& doesn't present any competition.

March

Ring Walmer & Wilcox re Jocasta's drawings

Weds Jennifer Cole
      Vernon Twiss } 4.00   (Mavis school run)

(veg soup?)

This is a meeting at **WALMER & WILCOX** to discuss Wendy's book and Jocasta's illustrations: Present are VERNON TWISS (Art Director), ALISTAIR GRANT (Sales Director), JENNIFER COLE (Children's Editor), MAX FURNEAUX (Editorial Director), SUE COMYNGE-KERR (secretary), BILL BEACON (Production Manager), & Young WILCOX, Chairman's nephew (Book Club Rights).....

Vernon Twiss · Alistair Grant · Jennifer Cole · Max Furneaux · Bill Beacon · Sue Comynge-Kerr · Young Wilcox

"It's dead boring waiting for Mum to get back from work," said Sal.

"I'm starving. I want me tea. I'll go and play in the 'lifts'!"

7

This is **JUST** what we should be doing now. It's **DIFFERENT** & it's **REALISTIC**... the vast majority of children see **NO** reflection of themselves or the world they live in, in the books they're given to read

Yes! The drawings are really ...er.. aren't they, don't you think? That touch of **OTTO DIX, NEO SUPER-REALISM**.. ...**GROSZ**...

THAT'S just what **I** think... they're **GROSS**, ugly...a **CONDESCENDING** view of the **LESS** fortunate by a middle class writer...

I always say to them: Write what you **KNOW** about....

It's not on! **I** can't give **STUFF** like **THIS** to the reps! **IMAGINE** old Tom trying to flog this to **HATCHARDS**!

And the art work doesn't exploit the cheap 4 colour repro deal we've made with the **POLISH** printers, now the **zloty's** stable

Ted Evans 230478

Ring Garage
Engine misfiring when idling
perhaps a air leak carburettor?
CHECK inlet manifold. Slow running jet.

	Chicken Pox	Measles	G. Measles	Mumps
Belinda	✓	?	✓	✗ ?
Beverley	✓	✓	✓	✗ ✓ ?
Sophie	✓	–	✓	✗ ✓ ?
Amanda	?	–	✓	✗ ✓ ?
Tamsin	✓	–	?	✓
Benji	–	–	–	✓

April

Wednesday — My turn school run. Trish rings — very depressed — says she's had a TOTAL PERSONALITY TRANSPLANT since Willy was born & can't cope.... spends most of day in dressing gown, tipping back VALIUM, trying to keep Willy & that enormous house clean. Promise to go round tomorrow & cheer her up. She says marvellous, as only person she sees otherwise is ADRIAN & we all know about him.

This is Adrian Smythe, ex-journalist, now a house-husband, and his daughters, Amy & Saffron....

Now Amy's 2, Moira's gone back to full-time work at the Beeb.

Amy

Saffron

Moira & I have completely reversed RÔLES... now I stay at HOME with the children & write my book in the evenings....

Adrian & the children drop in on their neighbour, Trish Wright for elevenses:

Oh God, it's Adrian!

WAaaa!

Excuse the mess, Adrian... I got off to rather a late start today...

Werr!

Honestly, Trish, don't worry! I know all about MESS now! I never realised before just how time-consuming housework is!

Don't you HATE doing FLOORS? I do. I have to do mine EVERY day to stop the GROT building up.

You know, people don't realise that housekeeping's a REAL job....

I must say, I find the chores tough going ... I tend to get up very EARLY & get the whole lot done before breakfast... that way I've got the rest of the day for the KIDS....

I hate saying "DADDY'S BUSY" all the time.

April

Poor Trish... of course having 1st baby at **36** & abandoning career are quite a shock NEITHER Stanhope NOR Jocasta do a damn thing in the house & Trish won't employ a daily any more as she thinks it's wrong. Wonder what Jocasta's like as a stepdaughter? T. says they get on better now — says Jocasta's got v. interested in GRAPH THEORY & sees some Cambridge Maths Professor.

April

10 Monday

Golf

11 Tuesday

Lunch Simpsons 1.30
Lyric Theatre tickets

12 Wednesday

Henry Portam Lunch
The Grange 1.00

13 Thursday

Le Gavroche

14 Friday

Carol · Chez Hubert 8.30

15 Saturday

Golf.
Willis, Cooper, Keighley

16 Sunday

Golf
Grooches · Drinks 6.00 ·

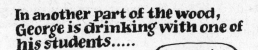

April

Week 15 PAYE WEEK 2

14

Staff meeting 10

Tutorial - Steve Tripp 2.00

Tutorial - Amanda Khan 4.00

15

Wendy's turn to cook.

16

My turn to cook.

April

Friday : My birthday. Children brought in breakfast tray. Nearly wept : Clay mice (made at school) from TWINS, BIRFday card from Benji & guinea pigs, hankies from Sophie & Bev, & frightfully expensive scent (Yves St Laurent) from Belinda. Lovely freesias & a WOK from George. WOK came with Chinese cook book & 6 prs chopsticks. All sang Happy Birthday round the bed. So sweet. George's Ma even sent card. Mine sent v. generous book token.   After nursery school, picked Benji up & went round to Diane's...

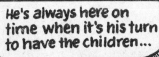

April

May

Sunday: Took children to TATE Gallery. George encouraged Benji to touch all the sculptures & then had a long ~~argument~~ discussion with attendant about what G. calls "Haptic Experience".

Tues. Street party Committee Meeting 3.00

✓ Sara N.   Adrian ✓
✓ Trish   Pippa ?
✓ Emily   Mrs Pope ?

Weds }
Thurs } G's turn School Run / Cooking.

Fri) G. working at Home.   P.T.A Meeting?

Besides lecturing in Liberal Studies, GEORGE WEBER also WRITES. On fine evenings, he does this in his garden:

The Neo-Megalith: A Structuralist interpretation of the career of Buckminster Fuller.

ROGER TIMMIS, George's neighbour, READS. He does this in HIS garden.

FUMBLE

Sometimes, husky Roger scrambles over the stout wall dividing the 2 gardens.....

Take a gander at THIS, Georgie...bit of ORIGHT...WOOrRR!

Well...not really my cup of tea, Roger.

No...now I come to think about it...she's **NOT** your cup of tea...little, bookish chap like you...big girl like her..... she'd want a **REAL** man!

Only kidding, George. Have some beer.

Look, Roger, I am trying to **WRITE** a **CRUCIAL** **ESSAY**....

NO BEER? *That* won't make you grow into a big strong boy! All right!.....off I go... ..here's lead in your pencil, Georgie!

Was that **TIMMIS** & his girly magazines **AGAIN**?

YES! A most **OFFENSIVE, SEXIST** periodical! He also made **INSINUATIONS** about my....

Oh, ignore him...those magazines are his **HOMEWORK**.....I always say *Those that can, DO*...and *those that can't, STUDY*

Look, I forgot, **THIS** arrived for you from Canada.

Oh **NO!** It's my manuscript!* McGill have turned it down!

* The manuscript is George's collection of critical essays, entitled "Weimar, Chicago, & the Cultural Squash Ball," featuring Moholy-Nagy, Charles Morris & Marshall McLuhan.

Listen, the reader says "Regretfully, the full complexity of your interesting arguments would be obscured by the heavy editing needed to bring the book down to manageable proportions.

?

Manageable Proportions! **FOOL!** Canada's full of **trees** to make into **paper**!

IDIOTS! CRETINS! Can't they understand the need for us pioneer academic anatomists? 5 years of my life **WASTED**!

Don't taunt him, Roger...he's had a disappointment.

In his anguish, George performs an act of Brute strength upon 600 pages of manuscript....

GRUNT!

Rrip!

Wendy & Roger go into BOGGLE OVER-DRIVE:

Bloody hell! I must get back to my **BULLWORKER**!

He could have **RUPTURED** himself!

My work isn't lost to **Posterity**, friends... I've got 4 copies at the **Poly**.

May

Monday

Start planning food for Street Party. Trish lends me book on
Cuisine Minceur — very healthy concept, everything low cholesterol: lobster,
truffles, foie gras etc. Très economical.　　　Anyway, I'm getting on
splendidly with my WOK.

Spend afternoon squishing up veg. in Mouligrater & make
1 doz spinach QUICHES. Shoved the lot in the freezer.

Belinda babysat. G & I went to cinema — Les Enfants du Paradis,
for the nth time.

Wednesday. Terribly worried about Sophie's reading — her spelling appalling too.
Met Pippa who said she can't understand why George & I bother
with comprehensives — She's got Rufus, Alice & Josh down for private schools.
(George is fed up with what he calls 'her weary, elitist lament')

Beverley has to learn chunk of "The Ancient Mariner". Luckily, she can't
sing it to 'Hernando's Hideaway' — doesn't fit, thank God.

Actually, I had a go in the bath & discovered you CAN sing
'The Ancient Mariner' to 'It happened in Monterey'.

Thurs　Working in library. George collecting Benji nursery school.
(my turn CAR)

Mrs Platt
763070
MRS PLAT-

Here is George taking Benji home from nursery school on the bus:

What an engaging child Benji is! How the ladies love him!

I drawed a pussy-cat today!

Aaah! How sweet!

My name's Benji.

Daddy, that lady's got *BIG BOOZIES*... *why's* that lady got big *BOOZIES?*

Look at that great big road digger, Benji!

Why has she got...

WHY has that lady got big *BOOZUMS!?*

Now look, Benji...all ladies have bosoms & men don't. Now stop shouting.

〉THINKS〈 This is interesting...Benji bestows on me, as *FATHER*, the charismatic & sacramental prestige of the *PRIEST*...we can see the passengers of this bus as a *CONGREGATION* taking part in the mediation between *TABOO* and *SOCIAL RATIONALITY*....

They're assisting at a *unique* moment in the *restructuring* of Benji's conceptual growth..diachronically...synchronically.....

But Benji has other thoughts:

THAT lady hasn't got *ANY BOOZUMS!* *Why* hasn't that lady got...?

Look, I'm sorry if my child *embarrasses* you.. he's coming to terms with *TABOO*...

Of course, in *ADULTS*, I would *DEPLORE* such *CHAUVINISTIC* behaviour...but *HE* is at a stage when differences between *MEN & WOMEN* are very ..er..*SIGNIFICANT*...

Why hasn't she......

Time we got off, Benji.

Why?

Must be a *CRANK*

Cling Film

Glasses

Ring EDMUND re booze

Remember Corkscrews/Bread Knife
Paper Napkins
Ramekins ✓
Pippa's Soupière

Salad Shaker
J Cloths

ICE?

Fri: Defrost Bread
Quiches
Pâté
Pizzas

Remind George TRESTLES/TEA URN from W.I.   Chairs - Church Hall?
"   "   collect old dears from Balaclava Terr.   Assembly Rms?
↳ IF WET.

Friday.

Went round to Trish's for tea. She was glued to Wimbledon. Seemed much better — said she was off Valium, said Stanhope was well & Willy was well. & Jocasta was.... Jocasta was having an AFFAIR — it appears with Stefan Torte, Carduelian Professor of Maths at Cambridge — Fellow of Judas College. Who'd have thought it — he's got children Jocasta's age!

Apparently he lives up the road from Trish & it all began when Jocasta went to see him about her graph theory — he's now helping her with Catastrophe Theory ... & other things besides.

Still feel rather badly over Jocasta's illustrations that W&W turned down (though do now think the artist they used is more suitable.)

Anyway, J. came in with her end of term project for art ~~st~~ school — she'd done an AD for MOTHERHOOD.

Join the Professionals:

The country needs volunteer (or willing conscript) **mothers** in the 18-28 age bracket, although there is an upper age limit of 35 for special abilities.

Motherhood.
A mother provides a **vital service** to the country, which often goes **unrecognised** and **unrewarded**. Motherhood costs spare time and the chance of travel. But it does bring much in return: the chance to develop skills & resourcefulness. Above all, it is a **challenge** and a chance to **serve** the country in a worthwhile way.

Raw material.
You may think we ask an awful lot of a young mother. But we aren't asking the impossible. All that is needed is the right raw material and the right training, during which, those selected often think they are going through **hell.**

Isolation.
The training is straightforward: the Health Visitor, the District Nurse, the Social Worker & the Media have to show the mother they can do everything the mother can do. Only better.

Combat.
Today's young mothers have got a **job** to do, whether it's holding the fort single handed, being in the thick of action in a playgroup or fighting dangerous household germs.

God bless them.
Men are eligible to join the **Mothers** too. Although they are not called upon for active service, they provide a useful backup team for the **breeding woman.** During her short service commission, a Mother is assured of a warm, patronising interest from the **Inland Revenue, the D.H.S.S. & Advertising Agencies.**

It's a good life in the Mothers and it's a **REAL** job too.

THE MOTHERS.

I think I may be one of the women you're looking for.

Name

Address

Date of birth

Please send me a brochure & full information.
To: Mothers' Application Centre

July

Monday. Letter from Kevin about our summer hols in Tresoddit. Says we can stay 2 or 3 weeks in Aug, provided 2 of us don't mind sleeping in little room above old gutting shed. Very keen for us to see his EDIBLE LANDSCAPE — — cabbage, lettuce, sweet corn, beans as far as eye can see - & ALL ORGANIC.

Tues. Most of Girls' school mates seem to be going to Majorca or Yugoslavia for their hols. Don't know HOW their parents can AFFORD it — esp. some of those families on The Collingwood Estate. Sophie says the Wheelers going to CRETE.
However, Girls don't seem to feel deprived. Asked them if they minded not going abroad & Sophie & Bev broke into song thus:—
　　"We'd rather stay in Reading in the rain
　　　You can stick your España!" (tune of Viva España)
Extraordinary. Where did they learn that?

Thursday. Prepare for Frisbee's visit - arrives Heathrow tomorrow.
　George says Frisbee's applied for a research-linked studentship at the Poly. Apparently, he's still into ethno-botany.
　Moved Benji in with twins. Twins objected - can't be helped. No spare room.

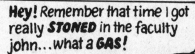

Tuesday. FOUL weather - really cold for July. This morning George tripped over Benji's trike at bottom of stairs & hurt his knee. (Small contusion) Insisted on large piece of plaster. We had annual row about moving somewhere bigger. Then G. stumped off to Summer Seminar at Poly, taking walking stick we use for blackberrying — said he needed VISIBLE SIGN of being MAIMED.

Of Course I would like a bigger place - esp. a room of my own. There's nowhere in this bloody house where I can write out of earshot of guinea pigs.

Tamsin & Amanda TERRIFIED of visit to dentist on Thurs. Reassure them.

Rang Jo - she's still coaching tennis 4 days a week. Decide to invite her & Edmund to dinner.

They arrive early. Twins tell Edmund about impending dental visit. Edmund undoes ALL my good work — terrifies girls with stories about 'the jolly old IVORY CARPENTER' & his WHACKING GREAT DRILL.

George brings Andrew Wingate from Poly School of Architecture back for dinner. Suspect Ulterior Motives.

Andrew has a plan for an extension..

I thought we'd take off the **WHOLE BACK WALL** & replace it with a **GLASS CONSERVATORY**....

Ah! **SCOFF** ahoy!

..making a **TEMPERATE** intermediate **ZONE** between house & garden.... we'd put **SOLAR COLLECTORS** on the roof... the **HEAT GAIN** would spill into the house in winter.....

you'd probably be able to **force** tomatoes & lettuces out of season ...train a **VINE**...

Like a big greenhouse?

It'd be **BRASS MONKEYS** in winter & **HELL'S HOT** in summer. ...ever been **FORCED** in a green house, Wendy? Ha Ha!

I **LOVE** the idea, Andrew - if it was **JUST US**..but the children still need..

Well, in that case we could make an extension in the **VERNACULAR** tradition....

We **STRETCH** the roof down to the ground. Then you get a **GALLERY PLAY STRUCTURE** for the kids, linked to the kitchen by a **spiral staircase**

That's **WONDERFUL**, too, but won't it be a teeny bit **DARK**?

Well, actually, the only true **USER-DEMAND** response, given the **PARAMETERS**, is to have your present **VERNACULAR** — commonplace materials of yesterday, in **DISCOURSE** with our own contemporary equivalent...an **IRONIC METAPHOR**, if you like....

— YAWN!

OBSERVER

Thus, we **FLATTEN** the roof to form a **BALCONY**... with a room underneath.. .. access from the bedroom - you could have a **MARTINI** umbrella up there - breakfast on the **TERRACE**....

The intentions of the **DESIGN** process are hidden in the **OVERT DETAILS** of **PERFORMANCE** specification...

Yes, it's easy to see that the classes of **ARTEFACTS** which continue to be made according to the **TRADITIONAL** methods have an **ICONIC PURPOSE**...

Don't **FUSE** your **BRAIN BOXES**, you **GOOD PEOPLE!** You can get one of **ANDY'S** last ideas from the back of a **COLOUR SUPPLEMENT**.... **D.I.Y.**..& **NO MESSING!**

SHERLOCK HOME EXTENSIONS Scandinavian influence! Weather Proof!

July

Edmund rings (sounded like from Pub phone box) to thank us for 'a very genial evening'. He DOES have nice manners, in his own way.   I ask after Jo — E. says Jo has a big day's coaching at St Leonard's Inter-Schools Trophy tomorrow — so would George & I care to step out for a quick noggin this evening? I decline — it's so tricky with babysitters etc.

The appearance of genial Edmund HEEP (& friends), in the saloon bar of the *Castle & Ball*, causes concern amongst those with more *delicate* fibres to their natures:

For Edmund was born under a very RUDE sign.

Evening, Squire! How're you, cod's eyes?

NOT scrambling ALREADY, Squadron Leader?

Oh God!

There is NO limit to EDMUND'S generosity........ .double brandies ALL ROUND...!

Now, what about a spot of BELLY TIMBER? Bangers, anyone? Scotch Egg?

Actually, looks like YOU'VE been putting away too many of the jolly old OEUFS ECOSSAIS, Ernest... look at that TUM TUM!

What a SHOWER!

TUM TUM!! I'll have you know it's a WALL of STEEL.. ...solid MUSCLE!

What say I PUNCH it, then.. ...HARD as I can? Bet you a fiver you'll say OEUF!! Har Har Har !!!

Edmund soon has his companions in thrall:

I say, what's brown & steaming & comes out of Cowes backwards?

The Isle of Wight Ferry! Har! Har!

And d'you know the difference between some PYGMIES & a Ladies' Athletics team?

Pygmies are...

July

But Squadron Leader 'Flapper' Noakes (rtd.), has had enough.....

Look here, Heep, I don't care for this sort of *mucky* talk.

Right you are, my old *Squabbling Bleeder*, ... sorry I spoke.

Whilst Edmund visits the little boys' room:

I knew a chap in the **Forces** like **HEEP - FRIGHTFUL PAIN!** Y'know how we shut him up? Bet him a **fiver** he couldn't get 3 **BILLIARD BALLS** in his **MOUTH**.....

...He got 'em **IN** but he couldn't get 'em **OUT!** Dentist had to do that! Ha Ha!

Be a good chap, Ernest...go & get some balls from the **SNOOKER** table.....

Thus Edmund undertakes a risky wager. His teeth are in peril.

Right! £5, Edmund, if you get them **IN AND OUT!**

IN!

OUT!

HOW did you **do** it, man!?

Simple: I removed my **DENTURES** as well. I've always had a **big mouth**.

Thank you, Flapper...in the words of the harlot: it's been a business doing pleasure with you!

This is Tresoddit, a tiny hamlet set in grey, granite loins....

Summer brings many migrant VISITORS to Tresoddit:

Some migrants throng the crevices up the cliff side....

In *wet weather*, the air is filled with their *wild keening* for a launderette and shelter from the wind.

Other, *SHRILLER*, migrants claim & refurbish nests by the harbour....re-naming them *"CRAB POTS," "Guille-mots,"* and *"OCEAN SPRAY."* Here they stay for a full 3 weeks each year, inviting each other for *GIN & TONICS*.

Here are *long term émigrés* from the city, who rescue bits of Tre-soddit from DECAY:

And here is a SON of Tresoddit, KEVIN PENWALLET, returned from the wider world of Polytechnica, to open a shop full of pure morally wholesome foods:

And bloody expensive it is, too!

Kevin

PENWALLET

PURE HIGH PROTEIN FOOD

The Webers are staying with Kevin....

When I first came here, this shop didn't represent a situation of ONGOING VIABILITY....

PENWALLET

PURE HIGH-PROTEIN FOODS

RICE BRAN

..local SEA & LAND-DEPENDENT nutritional customs were eroded by CAKE MIX and FISH FINGERS.

OILS

BROWN RICE

£2

HONEY

C. Levi-Strauss The Raw & the Cooked

Through this shop, I'm giving to Tresoddit what CIVILISATION has taken away: the ELEMENTARY STRUCTURES of NUTRITION.

Not CHEAP, though, Kevin

Ah, but NATURE doesn't CUT CORNERS!

At the Poly, I was FED UP listening to your abstract SOCIAL PRESCRIPTIONS...

I prefer INVOLVED KNOWING - like talking to old HAWKINS there, about his tomatoes.

LENTILS

Take old Hawkins — THERE you have a man who has never deviated from ECOLOGICALLY-DIVERSIFIED, ORGANIC HOMESTEADING....

.. a man who's in touch with NATURE & its INTERFACE with the SELF.

Here he is! Hello, Fred!

Marnin' Kevin - I brought my little list, dear

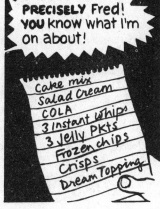

PRECISELY Fred! YOU know what I'm on about!

Cake mix
Salad cream
COLA
3 Instant Whips
3 Jelly Pkts
Frozen chips
Crisps
Dream Topping

You've collated a fine list of the major BIO-CULTURAL POISONS!

POISONS?

They're for our Joyce's party.

'hasn't got them as usual, Mary - lucky it's BUS DAY!

TRURO

PENWALLE

PURE HIGH PROTEIN FOODS

August

Thursday. Arrived home. Journey O.K. except Benji & Tamsin carsick.
  Had picnic near Exeter – saw lovely hillside, dotted with red & white flowers.
  When we got nearer, saw that the flowers were sweet papers, bits of old
    Kleenex.
  House seems v. small. Decayed lettuce in frig. drawer. Went to bed early
    with Graham Greene.

August

Sat: Benji → Josh's party 3.00

...As for Pippa's birthday teas! I don't know HOW she does it! She's made a cake with bright green butter icing, like a football pitch. The children only eat CRISPS.

Cassandra, don't take one bite out of everything! Finish what's on your plate.

Doesn't ANYONE want any CAKE?

Then the children leave the groaning board, & win MORE prizes. Benji still doesn't join in....

Oh, it's only a book!

No, we're going camping this year.

Hallo Benji!

Mummee!

..Eventually, the parents arrive & put away QUANTITIES of sherry.....

..we say our goodbyes and Benji gets a going-home present.

I'm afraid Benji had a TINY ACCIDENT... his trousers are in this plastic bag & I've given him an old pair of Josh's - don't bother to give them back.

I'm sure Benji's unsociability is a rejection of the nagging MATERIALISM of our society & his private WAR on WANT.

September

Fri. Trish drops in — asks us to party on Sat. to meet J.D. CROUCH (the novelist). Great social coup for Stanhope. Must say, I don't like Crouch's novels — the one about Essex in the Depression... 'Out of Flatley' — wasn't it filmed as 'Timberlust'?

Apparently, CROUCH now rolling in it, living as tax exile in Ireland. For a huge consideration has allowed Stanhope's Agency to shoot commercial for Instant Irish Coffee in his mansion.

September

Saturday. Mummy & Father came for lunch. Showed them holiday photos. Kids showed them their mosquito bites. After tea, Benji sick as a pig — too many plums. DUVET RUINED. Consequently, couldn't go to Stanhope's party. George should have gone on his own, but he disapproves of CROUCH.

Stanhope & Trish are entertaining yet again! Jocasta observes the preparations.....

Aren't one's parents' dinner parties **EASY**, nowadays!

Not that one's parents have **DINNER PARTIES** as **such** any more...one just has 'a **few people in for a meal**,' doesn't one, **Dad**?..

One doesn't have to **IMPRESS** people any more – **GONE** are the days of those **ghastly COMPETITIVE** meals: 5 pretentious courses, which take **ALL** day to cook & use up 2 weeks' housekeeping!

And isn't **CONSPICUOUS CONSUMPTION** rather **REVOLTING** in these **SOMBRE** times? Especially as one is entertaining **RADICALS & LEFT WING LITERATI**, this evening.

People have to take you as they find you, nowadays

Leave that dust, Trish! I don't want it **too** clean, or Brian will think we **still** employ a **DAILY**.

BRITISH SYNDICALISM
MASSIN/LETTER & IMAGE
Encounter   BODY

One just makes the room into a **sweet disorder** of cushions & important books.

Now, d'you think I've brought in enough **BOOKS**, Trish? ≶PHEW!≶

Thank God I haven't got to dress up!

Shall I wear a **JACKET**?

No, a jacket's wrong...

Perhaps a Turnbull & Asser without a tie...

..But Michael always wears a T shirt & donkey jacket...

..& Brian often wears a **SUIT**... Oh God! Help me Trish....

Now, the **FOOD** couldn't be more simple! ...completely without **ostentation**... some **sprats** fried in butter...a Spinach **quiche** or **2**...& a few odds & ends whizzed up in the blender, to make a **meek** soup....

FLOUR

September

Tues   Plan plot for a children's novel.
     Helped Sophie do her project: World map of DESERTIFICATION & ENDANGERED
SPECIES.   S. had further ambitions for map — wanted to add Nuclear Reactor
sites and DANGER ZONES for Plutonium leaks. Am very proud of her.
     George helped on Reactor sites, but was less good on SPECIES — otter, wolf,
whale, peregrine falcon etc.   George said GONKS were endangered species
— whatever happened to them? Last one he saw was in my Ma's garage.

Weds Cinema ~~Babysitter~~ ✓

Thursday   Look after Willy for Trish. She seems to be permanently entertaining
Stanhope's clients. She should make HIM cook.
     Jocasta apparently looking for a flat — sharing with other students. T. says
thank God, as J. being a right pain at the moment.

October

Friday: Heeps invited us for dinner. George tried to back out as usual, but put my foot down for once & insisted. When we got there, found Trish AND <u>STANHOPE</u>. Don't know How she persuaded him!

I do like to see Jo for old times' sake. She's coaching hockey & lacrosse at St L's this term.

This year, the Xmas pack of GLEN CRAIOGHDOAN whisky comes with a free calendar. Edmund's firm has given him one of the original paintings for the calendar, as an incentive bonus.

October

Heep offspring didn't make appearance.
Dinner was CHEESE FONDUE followed by CHOCOLATE FONDUE.
G. bilious in night.

October

Weds. George's late lecture.

Belinda at home with chill. Not surprised – she's always necking outside the front door in the freezing cold with that boy. Why don't they do it in the house? Belinda's got a perfectly good room. It's so FURTIVE & it looks so awful for the neighbours – They'll think George & I disapprove. Wish B. would get an INTEREST – like Jocasta or those HEEP boys. She just slouches round the house, pitting

October

the cork tiles with those frightful heels.

October

Friday: Shan't say anything but DO think Belinda's bloke is a bit much — effs & blinds & treats B. like an object. Awful thing is, B. doesn't seem to mind. So much for liberation.

Wonder what his parents think of him — though, as old Moorish proverb says 'Every BEETLE is a gazelle in the eyes of its mother'.

October

Oct 20th Autumn Fayre / Assembly Rms.

(Chutney?)

Father's Birthday = card.

November

Tuesday. George rather solemn. After supper said he had something important
   to tell me in private. We sit in the kitchen.
George says he has finally made an appointment to have a VASECTOMY.
   After 4 years of thinking it over.

   I am flabbergasted. But very pleased. GOODBYE COIL. I never thought he'd
come round to it & didn't want to pressure him.
   Suppose G. always felt more defensive than me about having
so many children. $\underline{\underline{I}}$ think people should be free to have several,
                   few or none at all.

   G. still looked solemn - perhaps worried about the op? Then he said
he had an awful row at the Poly today. That bloody man Pratt
has cut George's lectures on "Language as Discourse".

November

Saturday   FIRE-WORK PARTY

(Lentil soup
spuds in foil)

Soak kidney beans, mung beans
black eye beans.
Not too much chili powder

Tamsin Weber

✓ Pickles
✓ Chutney
✓ Ketchup
✓ Rolls
✓ French Bread } freezer
✓ Bangers

Sparklers
Milk bottles
Matches

Sophie → Warn old dears about BANGS
Ben →   "   street shut their pets up.

December

George's Ma rings up about Xmas. Are we going there this year? Heart sinks – remember last year – 4 days of George defending the Unions & comprehensives & Anthea defending Mr SMITH....yes, and the kids all had colds & we had a burst pipe when we got back. I play for time. Anyway, I DID promise Sara N. I'd join in her scheme of driving O.A.P.s to their families over Christmas.

George has to give a speech of thanks & a cheque to the canteen lady, who's

"As one of the longer-serving lecturers here at the POLY...."

"...it is my great pleasure to remind the Staff & students that, after 15 years' service, **Marie** is going to New Zealand..... and, therefore, things in the canteen can only get **better**..."

"I think one can say that, during **Marie's** despotic reign, **never** in the field of institutional cooking has so **much** food been left by so **many**...."

"I, for one, will not miss her air of **truculence**, her fault finding, her inability to give the right change...."

"I won't miss her **rudeness**, her **racism**, her **petty** economies & above all, her **congealing** food, cooked & served in PURE BILE!"

Go on! Take it! What d'you think I am?!

December

retiring – <u>15 years</u> of loyal service. G. spent most of weekend mouthing in front of bathroom mirror.

<u>Must</u> empty lint bag in tumble drier

Ring Sara

December

Monday: I feel <u>DREADFUL</u> - was in newsagents with Sara N. discussing which of the local elderly might need a lift or some help over Christmas - I think we might have referred to them as 'old dears'. Old Mrs Newby was in shop & obviously overheard. When I asked her if we could help, she said "I'm sure actions speak louder than words, Mrs Weber, but <u>SOME</u> of your words are bloody patronising!" Felt quite AWFUL. Apologised

George asked me what I wanted for Xmas. Last year he gave me a steam iron. V. useful, of course. Said I'd like something frivolous this year.

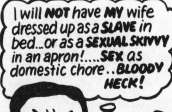

December

Order TURKEY

tin foil
mince meat
froz. pastry.

crackers.
sellotape.
gift tags.

TV Times
Radio "

GIN

Untangle Xmas Tree lig

Monday: Twins chirp up at breakfast: could I make them ANGEL costumes
ready for school Nativity play on Weds? First I've heard of it.
Thought that Amanda was NOISES OFF (she's marvellous at sheep) —
& Tamsin was banging tambourine.
Apparently 2 angels down with flu.

Mrs Gilchrist sends note later: could twins have <u>white</u> ballet shoes?
Spend afternoon putting BLANCO on their pink ones. Make haloes with
tin foil & wings out of old net curtain.

While I'm busy, Benji opens ALL the windows on the twins'
Advent Calendar, including Dec 25<u>th</u> — HELL to pay when
they got in from school.

Is it all worth it, I ask myself?

First published in Great Britain by Jonathan Cape Ltd 1979
First issued in Fontana Paperbacks 1982
Copyright © Posy Simmonds 1979

The drawings in this book have been adapted from episodes of *The Silent Three,* a weekly cartoon strip appearing in the *Guardian*

Made and printed in Great Britain by William Collins Sons & Co. Ltd, Glasgow